# Pilgrimages

# Pilgrimages

Poems

ANDREW J. CALIS

RESOURCE *Publications* • Eugene, Oregon

PILGRIMAGES
Poems

Resource Publications
An Imprint of Wipf and Stock Publishers
199 W. 8th Ave., Suite 3
Eugene, OR 97401

www.wipfandstock.com

PAPERBACK ISBN: 978-1-7252-5934-8
HARDCOVER ISBN: 978-1-7252-5935-5
EBOOK ISBN:978-1-7252-5936-2

Manufactured in the U.S.A.   02/07/20

To my dad who loves us more than he could say,
and to my mom who is a living saint.

"Prone to wander, Lord, I feel it,
Prone to leave the God I love;
Here's my heart, O, take and seal it,
Seal it for Thy courts above."

—"COME THOU FOUNT OF EVERY BLESSING"

# Contents

# Acknowledgements

Many thanks to the editors who accepted the following poems in their journals. Some of those poems have since undergone revision. I identified only those poems which have been published under a different title.

"Prayers for Shaped Nature" was originally published in *Presence: A Journal of Catholic Poetry 2018*.

"In Blinding Light, "In Mourning," and "The Splash of Rain Came First" (published as "The splash of rain came first") were originally published in *Dappled Things* in their "Mary Queen of Angels 2018" issue.

"The Pain of Truth: At a Lecture" is forthcoming in *Presence: A Journal of Catholic Poetry 2020*.

"Still Loved" (published as "Eucharist"), an earlier version of "Reformed" (published as "God's Eyes"), and "The Size and Shape" are forthcoming in *Dappled Things*.

"In Adoration: April 2019" is forthcoming in *America Magazine*.

I cannot thank everyone at Wipf & Stock enough for believing in this project. I'd especially like to thank Matt Wimer and Daniel Lanning. I'm still in disbelief. Thank you endlessly!

Thank you to all those who have been a source of support and critique, especially Jessica Schnepp, Robert Sherron, Sophia Feingold, Mary and Andrew Cuff, Jonathan Wanner, Bill Gonch, Greg Heaney, Benji Djain, Conor Hardy, Jessica Deal, Siobhan Benitez, James Matthew Wilson, Mary Ann Miller, and Ryan Wilson.

Thank you to all the teachers that have helped shape me and my love of literature: Mrs. Bales, Dave Wehner, Tom Bligh, Sr. Anne Higgins, Robert Ducharme, Jessy Jordan, Carol Hinds, Indrani Mitra, Mary Ann Samyn, and Taryn Okuma.

My friends, who are endless suppliers of love, support, humor, and inspiration: Anthony and Natalie Calis, Amanda and John Hale, Alex and Kathy Calis, Melissa and Rom Mascetti, Fr. Patrick Mullan, Luke and Edward Atkinson, Nick Sigismondi, Matt Golinski, Leighton Good, Jacob and Ashley King, Jed and Kristin Crook, Erica and Michael Beaumont, and Tony and Kerry St. Leger.

Thank you to my past and current students, who have made poetry personal.

To my children, Aaron, Lily, Siena, and Jude: you all have retaught me what love and fatherhood means, and how deeply they are connected. And most emphatically and inexpressibly, to my wife Stephanie. Thank you for your constant love and encouragement. There's no acrostic. Stop looking for one.

# I

## To God and to the Cloud's Edge

# In Adoration: Three Poems

## I.    STILL, LOVED

The weight of grace sits sternly over all.
Fallen man can fall, and break on broken
Ground the boundless imperfections of my being:
My failure seeing. My seeing without sight.
It makes the shards of life sunglitter, light
As a halved burden, cleanly cleaved in two.
And who am I that God should come to me?

The world is dirt made rich, Earth terraformed
Before we knew the term. For God so loved
And loved and loves the worm and all
Man makes is man-made bread, made stale,
And prayer, kneeling at the altar, reeling, frail.

## II.   REFORMED

The golden gaze
of the monstrance
melts you: Fire-
steady streams
seen reflected on the gold,
and there, reflected too, is you,
surrounded by a mess of carpet,
a knee-worn sheet.              Soak
the dirty rug, mud spoiled,
in the loving flood of God's adoring eye—
the anvil, and the hammer, and the fire.

The awe-inspiring Word, monstrance still,
and the broken shards of man
smashed together on the steel.

## III. THE SIZE AND SHAPE

The glow of gold in fire-flicker light
Transforms the white altar into God's seat,
Where I am compelled to meet him, round of bread
Dull dun, the sun of light around swells thick
As flickering flames, and God as bread sits
And devastates.

# WHERE CAN I LIKE JONAH GO?

Towards death       but there
is God. No way to
shut out his shadowed sound.
No cloud to hide me, shroud
in leaves my nakedness. No,
he is the deepness of the sea.

## YOU ARE

The unstarted start, the first beat
before the heart was heart, was
blood as wine as water as
soon as it was said it was.
You *are* was and were is and
are, like light long travelled
from a bursting star, alive and
gone, destructive, hot,
the untouchable flame that licks
a bush without burning, who rests
on heads, on tongues, who
yearns without words a yearning
strong as love, which you made
and are. The heavens and the star.

# THE BLACK HOLE CAN ONLY DEVOUR SO MUCH

When the star explodes, the hole
it leaves grows
smaller to
no-
thing and
its own light, tight-locked
in rock-cold black is
small and—
hollow
and quiet.

But new life is light in dark—
the quark-sized speck digesting all
until the Lord makes new
a bright-tipped star
from nothing,
humming out its song
into night

## ON THE DEAD WHO ARE PROMISED TO RISE

The Tabernacle fire burns away
the rain-dark morning, pushing shadows back
to corners. In airless silence, I hear Christ say
nothing. I see the flame, caged by black,
flickering, barely breathing its own life.
Thin fire, Christ, all time contained in now.
An eternity of deaths, unnumbered lives
all gone. And mine. It is impossible how

The Earth can swell to accommodate this loss.

How Christ can save the unseen soul but leave

the body. How promised presence sits in red

light, beside a silent tomb embossed

in gold. How time slips through memory's sieves.

Yet he must live, who animates the broken bread.

## YOU ARE

You are the time outside of time, first light,
alive in self-replenished oil, the olive branch
and tree, the fruit and fig and fire.

# GOD SEEN, SAINT OF THE UNKNOWN

*At Mass, Mount St. Mary's University*

Gilded with large saints
above the stonestern altar,
the enclave held
if space can hold a blue
so unbearably blue, Christ cru-
cified, arms split apart, a heart wide-torn,
wide-eyed death but beyond
                alive somehow if not now then
somewhen
                when he would already rise.

The blue churchcave, ocean waves
of color curling, curving in hues deeper than
space, in waves of holy thought
and Mary clothed in a different blue,
different how? A different blue.

I cannot love as you,
nude on a cross, rough wood aching
once-skin. In which
you were when you were.

Earth is empty, filled
with weight, trapped
in a linguistic loop:
unspeakable you who
make with words
the Word who makes
a priest who makes
a speck of bread
you, unstooping,
you who is and are
and was us,
who made the sea

and sky first
light burst forth
life bursting still
bursting through
death until the
unresting God
rests.

## DEUS EX MACHINA

Life whirrs. Knife-clinks of clunky conversations
heard through the walls of the English office, locked
at four p.m. (I'm here by obligation)
and stuck until the morning when it's unlocked
and school, unbarred at seven-thirty-two,
groans with student growth, with stirring,
with last year's alibis, and this year's shoes—
with last year's thoughts in this year's minds. Life whirring.

The chapel sits inside the school, a wooden
room: the altar, dressed in white; the cross;
the saints; the tabernacle table; the chairs.
The longdead roots that birthed these pieces shouldn't
share their smells, but do. A little lost
in time, perhaps. Now they fill the air.

# A LESSON IN GRACE

The shine of knowledge, first
fruit of the fall. The school
teacher, fact-laden, made
to make in God's image truth.
Already fallen. Already proven
wrong. Already mired in man's
language, the cursed tongue
that tasted sin.
            Then: Grace,
when God came as man and changed
a womb and a mouth into
a tabernacle.

# PRAYERS FOR SHAPED NATURE

May they glimmer perfectly like
Half real thread that ties
The fisher to the rippling water
Alive in its mysterious depths
Of black unseen floors and the muck
That floats up and the hidden
Tails that must move it
In thick unfeeling waves.
For this and smaller things too.

## YOU ARE

    You are the bell that clangs in muffled strokes
    in veins fish-filled with blood,
    a beat in order
            in order to fill
    a beat, sleet slow blood in blue
    rows moved and moving, a circle
    in unshaped avenues. You are
    the shape of love that swells as blue
    as the sea.

# GOD WHO MAKES LIFE AND MADE THEM BOTH

*For Danny and Jackie R.*

He unified their hearts before the first
breath of life, made each other's eyes
alive with sea-rich joy which burst
with beauty at each other's sight, the skies
alive with heaven's sound as heard on Earth:
angels' songs as heaven's winds, the fire
of Eden's guard—the sun, its unexpir-
ing warmth, its power, and its countless worth.

And in their unity, in God's small way,
he recreates the Garden at its start:
already large at birth, at time's first yawn,
he crucifies humanity's fallen state,
turns the sin of darkness into dawn,
takes his rib, and forms of it her heart.

# IN ADORATION: APRIL 2019

The quietness of time still ancient yawns
above the chapel, seat-still pews, slow stretching
wooden backs. Christ shining, Christ gold, dawn
in a fragile frame, eternal glowing,
naming every element in silent sheets
of unsaid sound, air living in its part-
icles, alive in movements too discreet
for sight, molecular, the holy heart.

In silence. But a silence firecharged as
a raging flame, untamed and quick as a match—
and in the cool air, has almost melted, has
already melted me. Has fast dispatched
the stone that builds my body, rolled back time,
has blinded me, and blessed with sight the blind.

# II

To the Memories of My Father

## WALLS: A PHOTOGRAPH

Dad was probably two,
surrounded by the balcony's cold metal rails,
to his left, a numbing stone wall.

The street was out of focus,
two stories below and almost empty:
stone too, cold and insensitive.
Despite the swaddling clothes
covering Dad from the neck down,
his head and face were exposed.

This was before Jerusalem blew up
into a household name
for reasons besides Jesus.
But Dad could see it coming,
He, the only one with sense.
He looks
over his shoulder
over the balcony-
rails around him,
fear there. The rails, he could see,
were full of holes.

Twenty years later, he left the city's famous walls,
hardened. A part of the streets,
no longer safe above them.

The face of fear in the photograph was real,
more real than the fortress walls
my father developed.

# JERUSALEM, HEART

My father's scars are too large for his mouth,
pronouncing words with British emphasis
beneath a Palestinian tongue weighed down by boots
some soldiers used to bruise his face. It was part-
ly his fault. He antagonized. He wouldn't obey
curfew. He would play with his band. Teenaged,
his rage was unendurable, the soreness of
growing pains, when aching legs feel bent
in places bones weren't meant to bend. The ache
of twenty years spent oppressed, now forty years
behind him, too far for aging eyes
to make out clearly, a blur of blood, injustice,
injury, and fear. He couldn't hear
so young. The undertones did not hone themselves
within his heart. Today his hands are rough.
*The work is hard, construction.* The loud turf
torn by metal teeth, my father silent.
I know a handful of his past, two decades
long as centuries packed down to morsel
portions we share at dinner. I know
the names of those he works with. I know the work-
scarred hands. I know he was not sixty once.
How quickly we would leave when dinner ended.
How thick are Father's decade-hardened walls.

## THE TATTOO YOU NEVER GOT

It could be any lion, but
now it's mine, like your name.
Like the shape my face takes
when I'm angry. Or when
I can't breathe from laughing, from
making my children laugh.

# III

## To The Shattered City

# BREAKING UP A FIGHT AT SCHOOL

A fight was in the air before the first
fist, when knife-sharp words were flying. We hunted
for predators, tooth-bared faces, cursing
in their heads, their unstained skin youth-stunted.
Unblunted words and hands were balled and thrown.
Our fingers bit their arms, held on, and broke
the fight up. They growled. Refused to own
their words. All show. Their arrogance all smoke.

Now, two kids expelled. Now the room
is frozen, dead in an airless quiet.
The only sound, the memory of the riot,
the shadow of the fractured fight, the fog
of yesterday, of history's vast cogs
turning, turning the class into a tomb.

# FIVE VULTURES SITTING ON A
# TELEPHONE POLE IN THE RAIN

When suddenly death was there too
stinking like a corpse in the car.
Tires' sounds cut through air like knives
and there was a flicker in life—a cloud

that sat on traffic like a reeking old
mutt, its musk stuck to the air,
its unproud head drooping miserably,
its breath hardly shaking the trees.

Still, they must have seen
some dead thing because at once
wings and wings and wings and
together they rose like one black bird. One

thousand wings all beating,
shaking the air in waves,
in waves like the old rug we beat clean
and sold after Nana Mary died.

The black storm of birds flew over the forest, fell
silent. Only the sound of rain on my windshield,
of my breath rattling, rattling, rattling.

The squeak and brief pause of windshield wipers
creaking over glass like mice caught in winter claws.

## The Splash of Rain Came First

### I.

The *splash* of rain came first, outran the word
for when the sudden gray makes gray of all
outside, and fall, and sounds are mute sounds lost
in rain.
               A walk home. A town
too much a city. Streets sweat, wetted
by the sky's monastic monochrome. A walk home.
               Puddles break
themselves as more and more and more and it is
too much now when puddles break themselves with their own water
the rain is not benevolent the rain is just beginning
when rain is sheetstrong is blanketing the windows
no is swelling to a hurricane to make of all things blank—
when rain is worn as coats are, heavy stains are
darker and the stars if stars were ever light are black.
The rain becomes mud music of the earth.

## II.

In baptism birth. In baptism
death. The logic rests with seraphs or
with God. A walk home. Is farther than
the ripple's outward rim. Is blind eye
telling blind hand it is dim. In
baptism birth. The surface of the city
shines as one. The puddles break, undone
by rapid swell and burst and one then one
after another and this storm is larger
than the gaping of leviathan,
the sidewalks choke and grow and sink and floating
for a second there are clouds but clouds
bring rain and rain breaks puddle-visions of
the clouds. In baptism death.

## III.

A walk home. A sweater soaked as flailing kelp
clings helplessly as skin, weak skin, and is paper.
The body was not made as ships are made.
The swirling noon is night now, or is soon
becoming night and footfalls home
are quiet calls, unsaid but not unheard.
A word can only do what it is told. Home,
or made like Moses to forever roam.
Or made like Noah's ship, of fearful frailty,
by him alone. Of every beast he brought
to rise with him, sway on waves made
larger by a voice—the unseen God.
The promise of a promised land is air
to Moses, held from holding to God's hand.
So water. So the rain. So every step.
So sinks mankind in God's enormous depth.

# HIS SONG, A SECOND LOSS

"One dead after smoke fills Metro station, forcing evacuation."
—*The Washington Post*, January 12, 2015

The metro train exhaled her death like smoke
and mourned—its every noise a dirge for days.
For days. The crackling intercom: no more her choke.
The metro hardly slows by her grave.

Some forget more slowly. A requiem shock
when a sad-eyed man's accordion begins to play
Dean Martin's "Sway." Respectfully, no one talks.
For her. For life that, moving, momentary, stayed.

He nearly smiles once. In solemn praise
he sings. His instrument and small chest fill with air
and fingers slide and roll and make their way
along the keys, an organ and a prayer—

Noisily shaking her cup, a peddler girl was there.
The actors left together, an abject pair.

# HOMELESS FOR THE FIRST TIME: AN INTERVIEW

The frozen stone seeped through browned clothes and sank
like teeth into too tired flesh. Here was home
for now, until clouds in thick dark threatened to rain ice
or until morning, when the library opens.
Sleepiness dulled him. The sharp edges of stairs were bones
instead of knives, and if he was alive, it was only halfly.
The wind which never left and flicked his nose and cheeks
reminded him of something indistinct. He tried to think
but almost slept, said to himself something bleak,
not unkind, no clearer than a cloud. Then the loud wind felt
weaker than he remembered. He had killed his hate for it
accidentally, or out of need. Like he would no longer stir
when his infant cried in her room. When he had an infant. And
he let himself forget but never made himself forget
and never really forgot anything but let it
slip off like the thoughts before sleep

# CIRCULATORY SYSTEMS: D.C.

Currents are trapped. Wrapped in steel.
Stuck, like veins, ducts that reel in, reeling
and hold in cold shapes the burst of life:

city, fake-motherboard-green, green
paint and green shutters huddle against gray stone.
Homes and avenues cannot move but still seem
alive, somehow, maybe, inside. The city is spread out and out and like
snow is thrown
from road-cleaning trucks thrown out and, thud, lands. Now sprawled
like a dead thing—
like fingers spread in death; hooked; stiff. The circuit closed.
The sidewalks stretch like endless legs to outrun anything
that runs away. The one-way roads close, like metal bars, frozen.

## THE SMALL

The metro's metal growl is deeper than
its tunnels, lowering its sounds like a jaw
and all who see are one and all who see are
wonderfully consumed.
                              The deep holes are dark
as death. They are dew-damp, tiles hard as dirt
hurt for light, ache for unbreathed air, are
trampled by feet or the heavy rattle of machines
that seem alive. These fill the station, or
the hollow, in its silence, wanes.

Each train is beast-brave, master of its cave:
The little gods of darkness, earth and man.

# WOMEN SPEAKING OF LENSES / ON THE METRO

How slow am I to see the roundness
of the moon, the rough rocks
dulled by distance, dulled by weak
eyes, weak at only twenty-six.

First week without my glasses, shattered
by my knee. (I didn't see them dead
in the grass.) Other memories
I would flinch to see

or see wrong, marred
by miles of months.

                       They are gone.
The women speaking of lenses
on the metro are gone too.
And I have already forgotten them

almost. *Hardly darker than water,*
*so I said the first time I saw*
*my daughter's eyes, thought:*
*how much you will see that I will miss.*

Tomorrow their conversation will become
general, a palimpsested ridge
dimmed by color over color.

Only her mother
will remember the night cries
and not always clearly.
Distance softens, a sort of lullaby.

\*                    \*                    \*

The rocks are rough against my ears and cheek
and stars are closer but how dark the sky.
How heavy my head feels; how dark the sky.

# WARMER THAN WINE

"Every time you smile at someone, it is an action of love, a gift to that
person, a beautiful thing."
                    —Mother Teresa of Calcutta


The heart sloshing with the ocean-weight
of grace—love as sea, love as blood
alive, as unseen cells in unseen veins,
or trees' leaves that drip rain in baptisms repeated
and repeated. Impossible
                    to deplete
this well. This gift of Christ-charged
love. This gift.

            But the strangers on the train        are
distances away. The gap of seats, glass eyes,
impossible to know in their cold shells.

Still,                          they      are not
immune to love.
            Only love has not
had them yet: seen them like shimmering glass.

# In Blinding Light

## I. IN NOMA

In NoMa, God is quieter than cars
or car horns; graves are louder than the deadened
voice of God. The sounding city sings of
her own death—. What voice survives this drown?
Can outspeak groaning engines? What sight outshines
the shine of chrome-glazed wheels? Light from light
is lighting up the rims of wheels, is brighter
than the neon signs or broken bottles,
is lighter than the darkened windows or
the violent steel that keeps shop windows
closed in summer heat when wind is
crying, kneeling at the doors, and crying
to come in—her voice goes hoarse. She stops.

The violent steel that keeps the windows closed
stands guard. Is stern. Is left behind when lights
change to green and engines only muttering
roar. *She looked*, each driver thinks of every
girl in sun-blind shaded glass, *at me.*

God hides, half-whispers. Is no match. God rests
each morning now. This quiet death would be
his only sign. So. Who can live here?

     \*               \*               \*

Who can live here? Two homeless men
in once-white kicked the shit out of
each other. A police car drove by blindly and
a white girl smiled too much, too nonchalant,
walked with her boyfriend seeing-and-not-seeing
the man who pulled at metaphorical chains—

the men who held him back: he demonstrated
viciousness. He yelled halfheartedly
the threats of death, his willingness to go
to jail again, to kill.
                    It was perfunction. All rage
was gone. But there were other homeless men around
who saw—who knew his practiced hate
that was for them. Who loved him for the show.

## II.  IN BLINDING LIGHT

If the poet can survive, he cannot stay.
        Each bottle is an *I* and he an *it*.
If he has heard the silent second that is God
he must leave now or drown in staying;
sound that floods the light-bathed city as waves.
He'll plod past streetlight-spotlights, the bright chrome
rims—center stage at every four-way stop.
He'll shut his eyes. God can blind, he knows.

He'll leave. His feet will leave. His mind will try.

\*                \*                \*

A sidewalk there is still stained with his blood.

\*                \*                \*

NoMa's poet tucks the voice of God
in the cradle of his chest. He bows
at the beautiful. He bears the bloodmoods.
He enters steel-locked shops and shops for food.
He's seen the face of God in pools, in wind.
It carries him like clouds. He trusts what he can hear
of God—the whispers. The broken bottles.
He sanctifies the streetlights' staggered glow
though he would never call it sanctity.
The houses he has seen from birth and known.
The chant of his neighbors lives in him.
*Do you know who I am? Then look at me.*
*Do you know who I am?*
                    nobody

## WHISPERED, UNHEARD

*speak to me of stillness*
root-footed flowers—flickering
wild showers of brilliant yellow—line
the driver's side of traffic-deadened roads
on Veirs Mill Road. Their homes are close to mine.

Their breath is smaller than their rustle
lost
    in fire- and wind-storms
    in suburban summertime
lost
    on me and
        whispered, unheard
        as we are
            propelled forward
        when the light for a minute
changes to green

# CLASS

*For Kelly Q.*

Their voices cackle, a gaggle of goose sounds
that drown all sound, a crackling of paper-
thin chats splattering like splashed paint around
the room. The sound refuses to taper
off. A cough is lost beneath their sheets of sound.

Their conversation is wild: a child moving
on before it knew it had arrived, and moving
into a different room and moving too quickly to
catch except in snatches that I cannot quite snatch.
I am no match.
                   But they are lovely as doves who
chat and chat and flutter off into their own sky—blue.

# BLACK ROT

*For Rian O.*

The stifled office air was cloister-closed.
It rose and weighed as neckstones on our lungs.
We complained. Of students. Of the rows
of unmarked papers, groaning like the song
of Sisyphus. *And it was very good.*
We made of mud a monument of drear-
iness, maladies of rotted wood,
manufactured as a sort of bier.

Once, Carol made a joke that wasn't
even very funny, but at least
it breathed its own life, sudden, fresh, and new.
At least it wasn't cloud-dark hate that doesn't
give of anything but blackness, beast-
cruel teeth. And born in brightness, look: it grew

# IV

## To The Shattered Self

# IN MOURNING

Dead leafless claws of winter branches
frozen against the starting sky, the newborn light
pink growing, somehow growing, toward red and life.
The branches cold-preserved, unmoving, limbs not
as animals in formalin-bloated jars but
as the incorruptible saint's body:

flawed and too unsettling,
posed in death, alive by clay,
too obscene for any word but prayer.

# HUMILITY AND POWER

kneel      kneel      kneel      kneel

feel       each       foot       fall

kneel      kneel      until     it's not

                             possible

to         kneel      as        adam     must     have

knelt      at        the       welt      of       earth

his        curse      and      kneeling was

a prayer   and      its        despairing     shadow

the        fall       that      cycles   back     each     year

kneel as   the       leaf that  rests   on      the      earth

falls       as        all       things   will.    *Be*     *still.*

The       sea.      The       waves.   The     Earth.

# What I Shouldn't Say

## I.  CLOSED-THROATED

Those sweet forgetful fish, the students,
Unnourished and stuck in bowls.
The bell. They rush out
Of sight into the glow
Of their cagéd phones,
These small homes, mechanical
Castles
Sneaking
Last glances
At the light
Before their eyes
Are warped
By the curve
Of the bowl
That wraps
Around
Them
Like
A tie

## II.   WHAT I SHOULDN'T SAY

They
Are still with me,
Close because
I love them and keep
Having dreams
(Nothing bad)
But I shouldn't dream about
Students
Should I? No, I know I
Shouldn't.
I think
They'll love
This lesson that uses YouTube
And when they don't, I pretend
It was for me anyway, and
I have a job to do.
So I lesson plan when
I should be sleeping
And I remember when
I should be sleeping how one time
I mentioned in class that

I am mowing the lawn
When this stupid wasp
Attacks my lawn mower
And I'm laughing
When a screeching pain rips my neck
And I slap and scratch and pull out three stingers
Already there and there are already more on my legs too
Many to slap away but I keep slapping
And I'm running but being followed by the ones
Still clinging to my ear and thighs that
Won't be brushed off so I just run like he-
ck.

When I get inside, I say, and am finally
Safe, well, I—then I take off, well
There are wasps literally everywhere
Even when—I mean (motioning
Toward my legs) *it was awful*
I manage. Ok let's talk about
Something else. Shall we?

# AT DEPTHS BEYOND

Your outsized grief reddened your eyes:
Deep signs I couldn't read.
You were asleep when I
Came to bed, the spot wet where your hair dried
And your eyelids were restless, flickering like a weak light.

\*\*\*

Months ago, our first
  Ocean trip together:
Shaking at the size
  So wide the sky
Seemed small
  And the weight
Of each crash irrationally
  Loud, the sound
That shapes the beach
  And rumbles. How small
Are two.

\*\*\*

What can the whale's weeping noise
Say of his wide misery?
Notes shaped by the slow sea,
The lived loneliness. His voice
Is only its sound. Who hears hears wrong.
Who sees sees undeserving, wave-forming curves
And first sight is re-seen—see twice the earth.
Leviathan's song.

Your long hair wet with mist.
You kissed each finger and my breath would not come.
Some sort of death, love. Another second longer was too
long. Our movements were our words, the bliss-
moments of noiselessness. The ocean swaying like a pendulum.
The sand, made cold by night, blue. It bit through
our skin. Our shadow clouded by the covered moon.
Your sigh was earth's and mine, sand, sky, air,
and ocean-broken waves, and night unclear.

## LOSING SLEEP

The dreams are mine, where death turns
every railway, every plane into cold tombs.

There, it is sudden. Losing whole lives at
once. Losing you. Losing you again.

In slow life, how long it takes. It lolls. At night
a firefly-lit field of faces, each love seen once, a flash.

When we died, it was the plane
that sank through air, kept sinking, hit the water

and sound stopped. And you stared. Eyes fish-wide.
Your sea-wet shirt a weed, now rounder than it was.

Love was in the only movement—my hand toward
yours. I woke gasping and was still.

We hid from our own voices. Couldn't say
but hinted at the size of death.

"about me?" *no*. "but him." *yes*. Left at that.
The scenes are mine. The screaming weight of night.

I know them like I know myself in dreams—
as fingers, moving slowly toward your hand.

# NEED

*no I need mom* my daughter mumbled
in sleep numbed sounds.
*Mom's asleep; but I'm pretty good*
*at cuddling.* It worked. She slept.

Then I was already in the sea of the past,
sinking in memory, its thick weight.
At my aunt's pool. When I was drowning. When above
me I saw shattered halos
of light and my arms couldn't reach the surface
and bubbles spilled from my scream which meant *Mom* and *help*
and *I need you.*
                    (This was before
she died.)

And her sudden face—muddied by chlorine,
her red fingernails like spears, but her face,
my mother's face, blurred and far
and farther, searing, glowing white, gone.

# DEATH GROWS UNKEPT LIKE WILD IVY

Actual mold creeps in each uncared-for corner
in the bedroom I once owned. The house does not show
the same neglect. It lives, is clean. Is cleaned
by my parents who forget the bones
of this room, buried in the basement, where moist walls
decompose—turning from sea green to black, each crack
teeming with disease, almost unperceivable, alive with decay.
My eyes are now burning—tears? mold?—
my eyes and nose, home to new parasites:
discarded shelves which weep their bowing weight,
now splinters flake from dried lines that edge
wood, unclean, water warped, an unplowed
field, a mess of fainting past and ugly forgotten now and film
on film of mold and filth and dust—a mask, a shroud.

This unfamiliar waste, this still junk
that bloats within the dying walls, lamps that will
not light and on my bed like some weak anchor sunk
into the rotting sheets a tire, flat, two, the rust fills
$\qquad\qquad\qquad\qquad\qquad$ the pillow,
a chain, a bike, and near, another,
$\qquad\qquad\qquad\qquad$ the air infected,
dust-numbed detritus, broken boards like hooks
and sails of fishscalegray dust that coats
old clothes wearing mold like barnacles on boats
a lifeless fan nests on my old shelves, homes
itself on dents I shaped in air I breathed.
My lungs reject the cloud that living kills
what history once buoyed me. Old books
$\qquad\qquad\qquad\qquad\qquad$ are bent,
no longer words but water-melted skins,
the drowning mess of my remembered life,
repulsive, unforgotten.

# THE FALL: ANOTHER DREAM ABOUT DYING

Through rough air, a body flew towards water
slow         slow       turns of legs
                              and hair and
eyes white as fish
in feverdreamed slowness.
                              The plane shipthick
had been on fire, three of four engines
power-thinned, bursts of smoke that
now spin upwards, or don't spin at all but sit
there as the plane drops and keeps
scratching the darkmarks of lungsmoke
in airspaces too far away to reach
or too ethereal to touch or
too blue, too much like
how metaphors are
thinner than air, like that
thing you know or
almost know or
know and just
forgot

# MYOPIC

In cold new January the
O of the nude moon and the
Hoot of an owl,
Its eyes round and unseen, are
One.

## ROCKING THE BABY AT SUNSET
## AND DREAMING OF SLEEP

The sun, setting,
rolling its head sideways
toward the softened curve
on the cusp of sleep
only to flare out
its light one more time,
turning everything
golden, bright and
beautiful as the
memories of you
in my naive arms.

# BROKEN SLEEP

Sleep's coat is on me,
its warm weight an anchor

as I sink into nightmare

sick-slick teeth and nakedness

as if there were a switch,
the light-flicker, nightmare's horn.

# THE WEIGHT OF FIRE

that firespark, that promethean spear
of crackling firewood singed your thigh
when you were five (maybe ten?) and camping

blind with pain you leapt (you screamed and screamed) but
wouldn't slide from the scorching skin
the widening black gaping hole
of crisp burned red sweatpants

until your aunt did

  and you stood shocked and shaking and
    naked (you were in shirt and underwear) completely naked

warmed by the stares and the humor
they all shared, but you were still blinking at
the spark that flew from fire,
the ash that must have floated up
like a lost leaf toward your eye

## THE LENGTH OF WINTER

Spring sleeps in rock-cold earth and will come soon
after the heaviness of snow heaves itself downward,
                                        down
with the bleak seat of blizzard weight,
                                a storm of waves, some
the splashing sea-spray, mist of waves
                                colliding, wind writhing—how
much is winter's night-dust swirl a cold smirk, impossible to place. Flakes
wasted as they whirl, feather light but stinging,
                                the bite of winter, white specks that scratch
shown skin.

They fall as one white sheet,
                        and how can spring survive? Sky sings
in cold wind howls, her vowels long and low.
The flakes are endless
until they settle like silence and end—a conversation dead.
And still spring sleeps in rock-cold earth.

# A Wedding and a Mote of Dust

## I.   AT THE RECEPTION

The groom's grandmother couldn't keep her feet
apart, horses tired of the yoke,
but tired too of fighting off their age.
They slid together in a rhythm she
might have felt, perhaps, once, when her pride
was in her litheness.
                              Dancing now no longer
made her cry. Her eyes were heavy, slower,
no less bright, but sight was seeping from them
like juice of thick fruits she could not bite.
Dancing now no longer made her cry.
She faltered, could not think the song
she longed to dance to—now no longer longed
to dance at all. Smaller than her size,
she watched from corners, poorly focusing
on anything in motion: the sway of living
shapes and colors rippling bright hems
and hands and hips and legs too bare and when
the dance was planet-swirling, girls
as beautiful as Mars, as how the world
looks from the darkness near the stars—
she unto herself would be the dust
that stays in stubborn cracks along the wall.

## II.  AT THE BIRTH

The groom's grandmother: solely
alive. Her kicks which used to drive
her mother mad are bursting as she breathes,
the oxygen she lives but doesn't know
flows through blood that tumbles, moves her, rolling
almost rolling at a month and standing
at five months, and dancing at a year.

## III.   AT THE COCKTAIL HOUR

The groom's grandmother wobbled in her seat,
would ask to eat, would ask again to eat,
with her full plate and her weak knees that heard
a beat we couldn't hear, that moved near mine
until she looked at me: *The groom's side, Nick's,*
she said, *I'd play a game when he was two,*
*scoop him, tell him, "You're mine!"*
"No, my mom's," he said. "And yours."
"And yours." *My Nick.* And she told me more
stories barely holding on each other's
heels. She feels another story, smiling,
didn't hear that it was time to leave
for the reception. So she stayed. Quietly
smiling as she sat back down. I hardly
saw.

## IV.  BEFORE THE WEDDING

The groom's grandmother's feet were toddling, sounding
their weak unbeautiful squeak, but she
was silent, eyes toward Jesus crucified,
toward the altar where she shifted steadily
now because a groomsman held her arm. His charm
was not for her, who muttered indistinctly.
He spoke to her while smiling at the crowd,
smiling loudly, loudly deferent, loudly bowing.
How much she hears in ears made soft by time
is inconsequential. He kisses the perfumed cheek
she can't smell and tells in words unheard
by her how beautiful she looks, and looks
around. The sound rebounds, goes crashing through
the mostly empty pews.

He helps her find her seat.
She nods. She smiles. The sound will not retreat.

# I SWAM THE CURRENT AND LIVED

I swam a hurricane and lived. *I*
*will not mention how the undertow*
*clawed at my heels and pulled my legs. And cold*
*bit my bones until my muscles froze.*
*Or that I looked beyond to miles of sea*
*and if I turned to look behind, I sank;*
*that frozen water killed my still-born courage*
*and I was forced to slink back to the shore*
*leaving Patrick deeper than I dared*
*to think: to waves or God or lonely death.*

*My body tumbled like the ocean knew*
*how small I was, or how immense its size.*
*As I was flipped, each gasp of air met*
*falling waves with chokes, with eyes still closed,*
*pushed closer to the shore then thrust straight down;*
*a slow death, I have heard, for those who drown.*

*I will not tell them that I swallowed sand*
*and sea that tossed me like a windblown dress.*
*I will not speak of fear or injury,*
*or how it vomited me on the shore;*
*or how I coughed and coughed and shook and cried.*
*I will not tell them that I thought I died;*
*I will not tell them Uncle Patrick lived.*

# THE 10 WAYS TO READ IN ENGLISH CLASS

Eraser in hand, standing in front of a wave
of faces, a sea of students. To say
anything is to break that sacred half-
silence, the moment between *what* and *is.*

He speaks first, with words as sure as his fist,
a finger-crushing wrist-shaking handshake, a smile
that slams. *That poem is*
he said *anti-war and its metaphors are as follows.*
I couldn't hear what followed because my chest
caved. Cummings trapped, "next to of course god
america i" flattened in the inanity of the internet,
pinned and wriggling to a wall of code,
stripped of its skin and waved as a flag,
ripped from cheap online analysis,
the first site when you google "next to of course
god america i analysis." It was the worst
sort of death.

*stop* I thought before saying *well maybe
not quite that simple* but
                            hadn't he won? Hadn't he
turned the storm of art to a sharpcorned proof
seated on a shelf?

> *And he said to the sea Peace! and Be still!
> Then the wind ceased, and there
> was a dead calm.*

This was still my classroom. There was still
time to right this ship. And so
we planted the poem and it grew.

Now, that poem is months behind us; but
I see it prick the backs of some students' eyes

when we talk about labels; or about the many
sides a story has; how no two eyes share
the same sight; how maybe both stories are wrong
and the right story is out there, wriggling in some gut;
and that's when I see a glimpse of that poem's roots—
when I catch them thinking, not quite certain
but just starting to wonder

# THE PAIN OF TRUTH: AT A LECTURE

Proofs, slammed as hammers.
Told, too rigid, sold as solid goods—
the clink of coin, the bitterness
when swallowed, the hollow filled with
steel.
        What feeler feels for truth
that lives between the synapses of cells,
uncelled, unsold? Unhold its loosening
reins and plains are widened wider than
the sky—its blue unchemical,
its shape unnamed.

## THE SPEAKER AT THE CONVOCATION FOR CATHOLIC SCHOOL TEACHERS, HELD IN A MEGA CHURCH

Passion, he intoned. His white hair thin
As skin. His bones already soft with age.
Passion, he repeated, to the room we're in,
All teachers trying to get on the same page.
All teachers being taught to teach by clergymen
And administration. The room is full.
They announced the few awarded, told us when
To clap. We sometimes stood. We heeded their call.

But I bristle. My room-enfolded elbows
Sharpen against the man on stage,
Honing words as weapons, minds as bows.
The lines of seats start blurring, bending cage-
Bars. I'll fight: I won't say a damn thing
Here. I'll teach. And there will truth's song ring.

# IN WORDS ALREADY DEAD: AT ANOTHER LECTURE

He somehow strides the skyward planes reserved
above the world for deep theology, Hegelian swirls
and history. He speaks of ages dead before his birth,
Earth-old days that lord as distant God. So well he thinks
he knows, he winds in his own reasons.

But his words are born stone-still. They stir not even air,
withering as weed-pulled roots, their smallness
unheard, crackling in summer's heavy heat.

                                    The room thirsts
for God's large breath. We suffer—
clutching under words that long to live.

## SOMETIMES YOU SURVIVE

No neighbor was hurt when the lightning-burnt
tree burst through their house siding. But you and I watched
the aftermath with half real eyes, the sky still
swirling, the trees still threatening to turn
our own house into—
by rushing water-heavy wind—

    Behold: I survived, once, the mountain blizzard's mighty ice,
    black paths snaking through streets.
    Behold: my hands clenched like teeth and thrice
    I slipped and almost said *tomorrow* but my hands
    were sure and, lo! I made it home. And, too, the night
    Pat disappeared, who sank, while sand
    and air tore at my lungs and my skin bled. I thought he might
    be dead, swallowed by the hurricane, already drowned;
    yet he sailed above the waves. How light
    he made life look. He rose like Christ, commanded me to stand.

Now, you, whose warmth radiates in lengthy wakes
of summer water, who breathes
in saint-sweet breaths a hope I cannot grasp, that formed
a world just we inhabit, of silence, or of speech without leaves
God left to us. Before the storm. Encircled by our vows.
Once, still secured, we clung like fruit to boughs,
our hands one hand, when at our first Mass, light broke
though the windows, flooded all the floor and shone.

# V

## When the Path Snakes Away

# Last Thoughts of the Missionary to the Sentinelese

*For John Chau*

**I.**   **DEATH**

Praise God, the venom
of the serpent has left me
alive, and God has given me this mission:
live and share him extensively.

Only, to the ends of the Earth, oh blessed
curse, the steady drone of missionary work.
The same smile. "Have you heard
of Christ?" They had
had enough of Christ.

Enough.

The Earth is wide, without end,
amen. And there is still the darkened island
diseased with the Sentinelese,
who cannot know him for they
can hardly speak and know
nothing but that ancient violence
of the spear. So. God has made
the mission clear.

## II.    RESURRECTION

Their arrows pierce my skin, and I cry
only "Christ!" and then "Christ"
and "Oh" and falling like
a felled tree I
wonder if
but
no

# SOME CONCERNS ABOUT YOUR HEALTH

The doctor is a quiet man. His hand
is often steady. He commands
a stern propriety. He loves God's brightened
path. He wanders

                  down it. And he's young
again. Alive and thankful.

                         His patients are the Lord's
creations, fallen features that he fixes,
Eden's beauty that he helps to heal.
And how he loves them all.
How he loves each one.
How he loves her.

               Her hand slips down
her side, her smile widens, his senses heighten
at her live electricity ungrounded,
herself a storm, typhoon-warm winds
that shake whatever base he thought he made
through prayer. He preens. She seems to like it when he
licks        his lips. How he strokes his own thin
arms. He charms, he hopes. She finds him mad-
dening, it seems. On some days.

He prays for her, unless
she is around. He dreams
of forgetting her, of
never meeting her,
of treating her
better. He gives her
discounts. He makes her
unnecessary appointments.

He knows that he is sick.

72

## PUSHING FAR ENOUGH

The movement of your warmth toward me—
enough. I was landlocked as a blizzard-
frozen city. Now, what weights I knew, I've lost,
a ghost-thinned hollowness, abandoned buildings
waiting for the crash of wrecking balls,
the falling, shattered shapes, the arid, dried dry-wall,
the heft that shakes trees' roots three blocks away.
Leaves shimmer in the winter's icy air.
They shimmer in the heat-thick breath of summer.
They move and move, alive, and vibrant as the spring.

# EACH YEAR IS A NEW WORLD

*For Gaby C.*

The flakes are swirling, making their own movements
in the cool air of night. The glass is thin between us
and them. It could be beautiful, except
they abuse themselves, are beaten on the pavement
like criminals. The cruelty of winter. The clean hush
of the cold. That was yesterday, I think.

Today, I see the snow with new eyes:
How the light beneath the lamppost
lives in each flake, varied, shattering and bursting
with the light of creation—it makes and again it
makes the world new, living with promise—
it could become anything,

                        and the snow-covered earth
warms like a blanket, like the first blank page of a poem
you haven't written yet.

## WHEN THE PATH SNAKES AWAY

As warm as summer soil, you leave
the room and now wind whips through
the wideness of the space you left.

As night is filled with your sweet
other faces—she is not
someone else. She jolts me, sweating.

As I turn, I feel my wife's small
movement,           closer.
I hardly breathe. I've never felt so small.

## THE WORDS IT TAKES TO SAY I'M SORRY

Look at how the lines of language bend—
or, hear it, see the sound in waves, the tumbling
of apologies. As they are said
they melt. They edge near anger before they tumble
into thin reconsiderations,
the self-effacing *maybe*, the half-hearted
*Ok*. Destruction as a poor creation,
us, unhappier, back where we started.

Is it as simple as *I'm sorry*?
I've tried. You know. But behind all words
are shadows, long-dead bones still marked with scars.
These down-weighted words are clumsy, if heard.
I pray to prophets, those who claim to have seen
a different plane where words mean what they mean.

# VI

Pilgrimages

## PILGRIMAGES: A SESTET

I wander, Lord. But in your wondrous grace,
and in your goodness, you offer other means
of traveling toward your light, and other ways
of pushing at my feet until it seems
like I was always aiming at this place:
A lesson—how to heal, how to see.

www.ingramcontent.com/pod-product-compliance
Lightning Source LLC
LaVergne TN
LVHW021615080426
835510LV00019B/2584